Isn't it Time Your Business Becomes...

BIZEASY

By Skip Williams & Steve McCrillis

Isn't it Time Your Business Becomes...Biz Easy
ISBN: 979-8-86950-586-6
Published December 2023
© 2023, Skip Williams, Steve McCrillis
Design by: Tara McCrillis

Foreward

I wish I had had this book as a Vice President of Business Development years ago. With it, I would have been in a much better position to develop business lines with the confidence of knowing how to grow, and in some cases, correct existing business contracts.

So, I'm delighted to have read this book now, as the owner of a Home Inspection business. This book and the Biz Easy Podcast is helping me develop and grow my business utilizing the tools Skip and Steve created.

I don't want to give away too much of this book, but I had the pleasure of working with Skip for a large non-profit agency for five years. Skip's main role as the financial and business development guru was to evaluate new business and existing business contracts in the areas of profit margins, analyze the financial health of a contract, and identify operational bottlenecks. So, trust me when I say you need Skip and Steve on your side to make your business Biz Easy!

Lastly, I'll give you a 7 Finds excerpts from this book that we all need:

- Find a coach that buys into your vision so that they are emotionally invested in your success.
- Find a coach that adds value rather than costs your company money.
- Find a coach that has a process as to how they may work with you each week.
- Find a coach that values your time.
- Find a coach that has been through failures as well as successes, because he knows where the guiderails are and can help you steer clear.
- Find a coach that remains objective, but not argumentative.
- Find a coach that values your intelligence.

Skip and Steve have been all of those things and more for me, and I bet they can for you too!

Kevin Abbott
Owner | Eagle Eye Home Inspections-Utah, LLC

Isn't it Time Your Business Becomes...

Introduction

Starting a Business is hard work! You will never work so hard in all your life as you will during a Business Launch, that is until... you open your doors and realize the hard work has just begun.

In this book the Boys from the Biz Easy Podcast try to make it "bizeasier", they break down some important business concepts that you may not have had much experience with.

Both Steve and Skip have more than 25 years each helping Business Owners build more profitable enterprises in a wide variety of industries. They have both owned their own business and have been coaching and analyzing businesses most of their life, with the gray hairs to prove it.

They have made mistakes, and they have seen the mistakes of others, and now in the autumn of their lives they work to help Business Owners avoid the many pitfalls, both common and uncommon. They write about business, they broadcast The Biz Easy Podcast, and they coach Business Owners every week.

This book tries to breakdown the sometimes-complex topics into easy-to-understand concepts which allows you, the Business Owner, to better control and dictate the bottom line and future of your business. From employee issues to start-up, to daily metrics, to sales and marketing, to exit strategy the Biz Easy Boys have seen, done, and consulted on it all.

YOU are no doubt an expert in what you do! This book will not make you a better Florist, Software Developer, or Plumber. Instead, its goal, and the goal of the Biz Easy Podcast, is to make you a better businessperson and to help you navigate the challenges most every Business Person will go through.

All businesses are unique (if yours isn't then that is problem number one), but the Laws of Business, like the Laws of Gravity, are not. Many Business Owners think that because they have a unique business offering, they are immune to some of these Laws of Business. But capitalism works the same for all of us. We all must deal with:

- Employees
- Government Agencies
- Finance Issues
- Cash Flow Concerns
- Am I making enough Profit?
- How can I control expenses
- Sales growth - Too Fast or too Slow
- Customer/Product Liability
- Networking

- Advertising
- Sales

...And Much More

For many of us, when we were leaning how to be the best Chef, or the best Auto Mechanic, we never had to deal with or learn much about these things. So, consider this book and The Biz Easy Podcast your place to fill in those gaps in your business understanding that we all have. And feel free to reach out to the authors for help on topics you may not find in this book.

We just want to make your Business Life... **Biz Easy**!

What Can You Possibly Tell Me About My Business

1

Thomas from Nashville asks: "I've Been Working in My Business for 20 Years... What Can You Possibly Tell Me About My Business?"

Wow Thomas, wrong side of the bed this morning? Just kidding. It is a question in many entrepreneur's minds. After all, you have come this far and done a lot of difficult things to get your business to the level it is including fighting city hall, lawsuits, labor issues, etc.

So let me ask you, if you had a serious legal issue, or serious medical issue would you hire a professional or would you deal with it yourself. Of course, you would employ the services of a lawyer or doctor, but here is the mistake we often make (including myself), we hire them TOO LATE. We hire them after we have a problem, and this gets expensive. Imagine hiring a fire department to deal with your burning business rather than a fire prevention expert to advise how to prevent the business from catching on fire in the first place.

That would be not only a lot cheaper, but much less disruptive as well.

To more directly address your question, YOU are the expert in your business. No one is suggesting otherwise. There are few people in the world that can tell you how to do plumbing, sell sunglasses, or whatever your core competency is, better than what you already know. But there are people out there that can fill in the gaps. Perhaps they have marketing or human resources expertise that you may not. Perhaps they bring a skill from other industries that can improve what you're doing. But, even if they can't do any of that, when they suggest something, even if it you know it won't work, you have better committed yourself to your process and removed all doubt that what you are doing works best. You have a sounding board that allows you to talk through an issue before reaching a conclusion.

I would encourage every business owner to have a mentor, a coach, a consultant, that can work with them on a regular basis so that you can be even stronger. Just like athletes that have played the game for 20 years, they constantly work on improvement, else they plateau, or worse, fade away.

Clowns to the left of me, jokers to the right:

I am only exaggerating a little bit when I say that running a business is the loneliest of jobs. On one side of you there are customers that want everything for free. Employees that think all their problems, especially the financial ones, are YOUR problem to fix. On the other side you have Creditors that think they should be paid before you, and debtors that think you should/can wait for money that is rightfully yours. Not to mention

Government agencies, COVID restrictions, the tax man and other bureaucracies, but don't get me started on that can of worms.

The point is, what you face each day is overwhelming, and if you are doing it alone it beats you down and takes you away from those things that can help build your business to the next level. A coach, or confidant helps you refocus and stay more focused on the things that add value to your business. The distance from the day to day allows this person to have a different perspective than you. Not because he or she is smarter, but rather focused on YOUR vision instead of all the noise, much like an athletic coach can.

- Find a coach that buys into your vision so that they are emotionally invested in your success.
- Find a coach that adds value rather than costs your company money.
- Find a coach that has a process as to how they may work with you each week.
- Find a coach that values your time.
- Find a coach that has been through failures as well as successes, because he knows where the guiderails are and can help you steer clear.
- Find a coach that remains objective, but not argumentative.
- Find a coach that values your intelligence.

Lastly Thomas I would like to say that you would be surprised how much a good coach can tell you. Often times, with some simple financials and little else I have been able to steer owners away from a huge financial mistake as well as guide them, through a series of questions, to brand new revenue channels, or huge process improvements. I am able to do this not by knowing more than the business owner but rather by learning from him or her and then seeing something that they may have missed or not thought important. I like to think that I am helping to amplify the skills and intelligence that the business owner already has.

Putting Out Fires 2

Barbara from Nevada asks; "How can I get to a point where I am managing my business instead of putting out fires?"

Thank you for your candor. It is greatly appreciated, and you aren't alone. I'm sure you've heard the expression, "if I had a nickel..." In this case the subordinate clause is, "for every time a business owner has told me that they spend most of their time fighting fires in their business." My response has become part of every meeting with a business owner who may well have his schedule in order but continues to deal with operational interruptions. Put simply, a business owner should never resort to being a babysitter, a policeman or a firefighter. As I say this, most respond with laughter or at least a smile. Turns out that most owners find themselves doing exactly that. Babysitting employees who can't seem to get along, department heads and/or vendors who need a mediator and/or staff who want YOU to solve all their problems.

But why? I was told early in my career, fortunately, that you should never go to your boss with problems, only solutions. All too often a business owner will unwittingly answer every question posed by an employee, or worse, a department director immediately when asked and then the owner grumbles about having to put out fires or babysit, all day long. In the employee's mind, the easy solution is to ask YOU the question rather than risk doing it wrong. Let's face it, depending on what kind of a culture was developed in the company, this easy answer is typically the "go to". In most cases, an employee knows the answer but fear of retribution or pure laziness, they seek validation in any way they know how. That is typically to ask you.

Years ago, Scandinavian Airways had a problem that I believe most companies have when dealing with the front line, customer conflict. To abbreviate the story, ticket counter attendants had no authority to change, adjust or refund fares for passengers with traveling conflict. This was obviously quite unnerving to passengers. If you've ever traveled by air and have had to interact with the ticket agent, you can imagine the anxiety. Through serious examination, review and overhauling the decision-making authority, the company granted more "on site" decision-making authority to the front-line representatives. In a year's time, the company doubled its bookings and received AAA rating for customer service and passenger care.

Starting with clearly defined job responsibilities, levels of authority and a clearly defined organizational flow chart, the solutions become clearer. These are all part and parcel of developing effective operational flow and developing strong team members. Who is that employee's direct report? What decision making authority do they have? Do they have a fear of their supervisor blowing up if something goes sideways or are they encouraged to think it through and provide solutions in future situations? There's your culture kicking in AND providing solutions. Every time I have been with the owner, and I hear him respond with a quick answer, I always ask him, "how often do they ask you those kinds of questions?" Typically, the owner will say, "all the time!" How about this approach... ask them what THEY would do? Listen to the answer, agree to their response, or guide them through to the solution and applaud them (figuratively), and encourage them to proceed. What happens in this case? The employee slowly learns the value of decision-making, averts the conflict, gains confidence – everyone wins. It's a process that takes time and patience to implement but in the long run you gain confident, more competent team members.

As for policing and babysitting... a review of company policy is probably a good start. You as a business owner and likely the one who started the business on your own, you absolutely recognize the nuances and details of the work you provide and the service you perform, intimately. As a business owner myself, I have realized that as my staff grows it is easy to assume that all the history and circumstances of previous work is somehow understood by all incoming staff members. I've learned that couldn't be further from the truth. As your company evolves, it is a great idea to review process, procedure, and workflow changes with existing and incoming staff for understanding and compliance. Your staff wants to do a good job and be successful. Providing them with proper on-boarding, contemporary guidelines, and measures of what acceptable and exceptional performance looks like is essential for them, and you, to be successful.

As a company who works with businesses to help craft effective means to grow a company's staff and improve overall effectiveness as they shift from being "firefighters" to business leaders, I can tell you with assurance the results are ultimately rewarding. I have confidence that "working on the business" vs "working in the business" will give you great peace and your customers confidence in referring you to others.

Manager to Leader

Steve from Montana asks: How do I transition from Manager to Leader in my business?

What an important question Steve. This is critical to taking your business to that "next level" and NOT transitioning is a mistake that many business owners make that stagnates the growth of that company, and never allows them to realize their vision.

First let me say congratulations for achieving some level of success. It sounds like, through hard work and late nights you have managed to build your business to some level of respect within your industry. And you are wise to realize that to continue to grow you must step back from working on the day-to-day issues and begin work on the consistent long-term growth of the business.

Just like Al Pacino said in The Godfather: "Just when I thought I was out, they pull me back in!"

There will be many distractions (you are probably encountering them now) that will suck you back into the day-to-day challenges. You must fight to minimize this!

Perhaps it is time to hire a manager to become that buffer, perhaps it is better training so that your employees can make more of the decisions. But whatever solution that you come up with, it will probably go against your natural instincts that now require you to be involved in every decision. That ego that it took to get into, and build your business this far, is what you need to fight against in order to find a NEW happy place that allows you to set the vision for your company and inspire your Lieutenants to execute that vision.

Inspire and influence will now replace sell and demand. You will need to focus on how to increase sales while they work on building a better operation. You will be deal-making, rather than turning the wrench. You will work in broad strokes, instead of dealing with details. So, as you can imagine, it is critical to build a strong, capable team to surround yourself with. A "What's next Boss?" type direct report employee is no longer going to cut it.

So, Step #1 is to build a good team that can work more autonomously and Step #2 is to change your mindset and work on those things that will provide long term, sustainable growth.

Not easy, is it Steve? But it is critical. So, think about it this way; Pareto said that 80% of results come from 20% of your effort.

This is a good illustration of what you are probably doing right now. In effect, you are spending 80% of your time managing (or perhaps even as a technician), and 20% being a Leader, working on the long-term benefit of your business. Imagine that next week you worked on the good stuff 30% of the time, and next month you worked 40% on these critical tasks and eventually you have reversed the equation to 80% of the time you are working on the deal making, sales increasing, infrastructure expansion that your business desperately needs.

Building a business is one of the hardest things you will do in your life and the skill sets needed will change at various points in your journey.   We also know that if transition never happens, not only will the business stagnate, but the owner will most likely burn out. This is one of those things that consulting an advisor or expert can provide exponential gain.

Pricing Goods and Services 4

Jean from Texas asks: Do You Have a Good Method for Pricing Goods and Services?

Thanks for asking this Jean, Pricing is one of my favorite topics. It is a topic that seems complex but it doesn't have to be.

First let's establish whether we need to price by the SKU or price by the UNIT. If your company makes a specific product or provides a specific service that always has the same scope of work then we need to price by the SKU. Other products and services however, need to be priced by the hour, minute, pound, foot, etc.

Whether pricing by SKU or UNIT the method used is the same, the difference is, one is a commodity with a "catalog" price, and the other usually requires you to provide estimates and/or quotes to your customer.

Next, let's understand that pricing is a two-part calculation. The first part is calculating what your company can "afford" to sell the product or service for (see below). And the second is understanding what the market will pay for that product or service. When you have both numbers, you will then know if your business (or this product line) is viable. Obviously, if the first number is larger than the second the venture is not feasible, and conversely if it is less than the second you have opportunity.

The Method:

Most of you know how to estimate your time and materials to calculate your "raw cost", I would encourage you to also add other variable expenses that can also be estimated on a per SKU/UNIT basis. Those might be products or services that consume large amounts of energy, sales commissions, online sales fees, employer's share of taxes, benefits, etc.

Once we have established the "raw cost" we then need to add "burden" to that cost. In order to do that we will need to look at your Profit & Loss Statement and separate your fixed expenses (overhead) from your cost of goods or services (COGS) or variable expenses.

When we have the total cost of overhead (again those expenses that have nothing to do with producing the product or service) we need to divide that by the COGS to obtain the burden rate. YES, I said divide by COGS NOT total revenue. It is a common mistake to look at overhead as a percentage of revenue BUT we need to remember that we are working from raw cost toward the final price (revenue) so we need a rate that we can add to our cost of goods.

Let's say for example that our percentage is 50% we would then multiply our raw cost by 1.50. This new number is what we could afford to sell our product/service for that would cover our costs and overhead.

Next, we need to answer how much profit margin we would like to make. This can be found by looking at industry averages or simply what you think is fair (and competitive).

Lastly (part 2), we need to compare this price against what our competitors are charging. You will want your price to be competitive, so you may want to adjust up (never down) accordingly.

A few things to beware of:

When adding your profit margin, we need to convert that number to "markup" as margin works from price to cost, markup works from cost to price. Example for a 10% profit margin here is the formula to convert to markup: $(100*.10)/(100-(100*.10)) = 11.11\%$

Be careful with industry average margins as they are usually based on raw cost not fully burdened cost.

Overhead as a percent of COGS will vary as your business grows (or shrinks) and should be recalculated when revenue changes dramatically. This is also one of the hurdles that must be overcome in a start-up situation or product launch. When this happens, I recommend using projected costs. Project the costs to a reasonable point in time when sales are/will be a year from now.

As revenue grows and overhead remains the same, the cost to deliver your product or service go down and amplifies your bottom-line profit, giving you more ability to flex your muscles with your competition.

Pushing the price thresholds should be a consideration, but we can talk about that later when we talk about price increases.

The Right Person for the Right Job **5**

Did you ever notice, either in your own business or when visiting another business, that some employees love what they do, and others wish they were not there, or struggle to be competent?

Do you wish everyone that you employed were happy and productive, or do you take the attitude that you are not paying them to be happy?

I think the days of the "not paying them to be happy" are over. I am not saying you can't be tough and demanding, but at the end of the day if your employees are not happy you will pay for that in a hundred different ways without even knowing it. They might include:

- Theft
- Not friendly with customers
- Not concerned with quality
- Apathy
- No pride or job ownership

- Backstabbing you or other employees
- And scores of other "creative" ways that we haven't even thought about

A lot of this can be due to a toxic workplace culture, but I am going to save that topic for another day, because the start of having happy employees starts with hiring employees with the right fit for the job.

Hiring someone just because they are willing, is not enough. You do him/her no favors by hiring them into a job that ultimately does not fit them. More importantly when their unhappiness turns to resentment, extricating them from that job is usually very painful, and more often than in years past can end up in litigation or the involvement of state agencies.

So, it makes sense to have "the right butts in the right seats" and to never settle for marginal applicants. But how do we make sure we have a good applicant sitting in front of us at that interview?

All too often employers start an interview by asking a question or two and then begin telling the applicant about the company or themselves, ultimately taking over the bulk of the conversation. This "telegraphs" the responses that the employer is looking for and after he/she nods their head a couple of times and agrees with the interviewer, the interviewer begins to believe that this person is exactly what the company needs and perhaps sees a younger version of themselves in the candidate. We call the this "the halo effect".

So how do we avoid this pitfall?

By creating a set of questions, unique to that position, that you ask to all the candidates. These questions are designed to draw more and more information from the candidate by being open ended and with follow up questions like "tell me more about that" or "tell me about a time that..." or "how did this make you feel".

But before we can design the questions, we first must know what characteristics we are looking for. And the characteristics we need for one job description (Janitor) may not be what we are looking for in another (Teacher).

So, each Job Description should have its own set of questions that search for the characteristics that you are looking for. And we determine that by looking at other employees with the same job title.

Think about the good employees that do that job, and what separates them from the marginal employees. Why do they enjoy the challenges that the job presents, while others do not? What makes them special or a perfect fit?

Once we understand those characteristics, we can then design questions that help us determine whether the candidate has similar ones.

This process can take a couple of days of observation and a couple hours to complete the questions, but if it saves you just one lawsuit, or some employee sabotage, then it is time well spent.

Like most tasks in a business, they need to be turned into a process and then memorialized. This takes away the subjective nature of an interview and begins to turn it into a scientific or mathematical endeavor that provides a much higher degree of success. Not to mention a more valuable/saleable business.

Speaking of scientific mathematical hiring processes, I am working on an even more scientific method right now. And I am looking for a couple of companies to Beta test. It takes a simple Myers Briggs personality test and charts the results against the "top performers" for that job so that you can see if the person you are interviewing has the natural talents, aptitude, and personality necessary to perform well at this job. If you and your company are interested in helping me to perfect this tool, please reach out to me.

That said, Interviewing should not be an art, a hunch, or a good feeling unless you are just looking for a lunch buddy. Rather it should be as standard, and scientific as possible so that you can easily compare one candidate to another later by referring to your notes. And ALWAYS pay attention to those red flags that often pop up during an interview.

Lastly, make sure you never do more than 10% of the talking, do not "telegraph" your feelings about their answers, and the time to "sell" them about your company and why they should take this job is later when you have decided that this is the candidate you really want.

Using Your Financials for Better Decision Making 6

"If you treasure it, you should measure it!" This old adage is more commonly known among bookkeepers and financial consultants. Not to throw accountants and CPA's under the bus, but their primary concern is to be able to prepare a tax return at years end for you to see how much taxes you may owe. It's kind of a backward thinking proposition. But shouldn't YOU know if you're making any money WHILE you're making it?

Let's use your car as a metaphor here; how do you know if you're low on gas? If your car is running too hot? If your oil pressure is at a dangerous level that might shortly damage the engine? You look at your dashboard. There is a series of lights and gauges that help you decide when something is okay or worse, if something isn't. It provides you with information to make a decision; get gas soon, add coolant to your radiator or add oil. In your business, your "dashboard" is your accounting system, if it is set up properly.

If you use QuickBooks or any small business accounting system there are several reports that you can download or look at. There are 2 major reports that every business owner should pay attention to.

The Balance Sheet gives us a snapshot of our business at any point in time. We look here typically to see our bank balances, accounts receivable (who owes us money), and our accounts payable (who we owe money to). I won't spend a lot of time on Balance Sheets but a balance sheet can also tell us how much equity the business has by subtracting Liabilities from the Assets.

But most of the day-to-day decision making can be done by knowing how to analyze the P&L a.k.a. the Profit and Loss Statement or the Income statement.

The P&L tells us what has happened over the course of a period of time. It tells us what revenues we earned, how much we spent to get those revenues, and how much we spent on our overhead.

While typical periods of time to look at may be a month, quarter, or year they can be run for any custom time period you need. This was not always true, because in the old days we posted and closed our books each month. But QuickBooks and other accounting programs, if kept up to date each day, will provide accurate reports for a week period, 10-day period, or whatever you need or desire.

The first part of the P&L shows us all of our Revenue or the proverbial "Top Line". There may be more than one type of revenue as you will often see Sales Revenue, Interest Revenue, and Other Revenue. But there may be other types of revenue as well. In fact, if your business has very different types of Sales Revenue, for example you do printing, but you also sell advertising I would recommend having a revenue line for each. Because, as we are about to talk about, they have very different costs associated with each type of revenue.

The second part of the P&L shows us our expenses, and if we set our accounting up properly it will show both COGS (Cost of Goods Sold, or also more recently known as Cost of Goods and Services) which is also known as Variable Expenses, and our Fixed Expenses, also known as Overhead.

The reason it is important to have these two things segregated is so we know how much it cost to serve our customer with goods and/or services (labor, materials, etc.), and how much it cost just to have our doors open for business (rent, insurance, management labor, etc.).

If your P&L does not reflect COGS and Fixed Expenses separately you may want to work with your bookkeeper to fix this issue. Without the segregation your books are good for tax purpose, but not very useful for managing your business.

The last part of the P&L is the Profit (Loss) line, or "The Bottom Line" which tells us during this period how much money was left from the Top Line Revenue after we paid the Variable and Fixed Expenses, and may be a negative number if we did not bring in enough Revenue or we paid too much for some Expenses.

Sniff Test:

When I look at a P&L I first look at the Fixed Expenses to see if any of them are significantly different than in previous months. If they are, then then I immediately look into finding out why. I also look at each line of Fixed Expenses periodically to see if we are paying for "want to haves" or "need to haves" or for alternative sources that may be cheaper.

Next, I look at Variable Expenses or COGS. To look at these properly we cannot compare to other months on a dollar-to-dollar basis, we must first convert the dollar amount to a percentage of revenue.

Word of caution here: If you have several types of revenue that are significant or material then rather than dividing the expense by the Total Revenue, you should divide by the corresponding Sales Revenue that created those COGS expenses. This will provide the most accurate picture of what it cost to create those sales.

Once you have an accurate percentage for each of the COGS expenses, then you can compare those percentages to other months to see if something is JDLR (Just Doesn't Look Right).

A simpler way to track this is with the Contribution Margin method. Here we take the total of our COGS and divide by the corresponding Sales Revenue to obtain how much it costs us to make a dollar. We then reverse that by subtracting that amount from a dollar to find out how much we keep out of every dollar before considering Overhead.

Simple example:

Total Revenue for period = $100,000

Total COGS for period = $65,000

Therefore, it costs us $0.65 to make $1.00

Or put differently we keep $0.35 out of every Sales Revenue dollar to pay our Overhead and contribute to Profit.

The reason I like the Contribution Margin calculation is:

- I can track it each month and compare to see if our operations are getting more or less efficient.
- I can do the calculation mid-month (usually matching a pay period).
- I can use the Contribution Margin to divide into my Overhead to obtain my Break-Even
- I can determine how many Revenue dollars (additional sales) it will take for me to pay for a rent increase, a new hire, company car, new computer, etc.
- I can share the number with department heads or line personnel to provide a measure of efficiency.
- I can use it in my ROI calculations for investing in a new piece of equipment.
- I can use it in calculating pricing for goods and/or services.

For people who hate numbers, as well as people like myself that enjoy the numbers, this can be the most useful "One Number Tool" for managing your business.

Last Thoughts:

After all the money you spend to keep the books up to date, wouldn't it be nice to have them be a very useful tool that helps you manage your business, rather than an expense just to have accurate taxes?

Information is ONLY as good as the decision you can make from it. With this brief overview of the key performance indicators from your P & L and balance Sheet, you can make more informed decisions about the operation of your business. After all, it's not how much you make, it's how much you keep!

Take it from someone who hates accounting, you don't need to be an accountant to make good use of your accounting. It costs the same amount of money to keep your books up to date as it does to do it all at the end of the year for the Tax Man (and maybe less). So why not get a better return on the accounting expense by making sure it is a useful tool for your day-to-day decision making.

The Physics of **7** Business

While creativity and uniqueness are wonderful things, especially in business because it separates you from your competition, it sometimes leads us to believe that normal or standard business principles do not apply because of that uniqueness.

Think of business as you would think of Physics. In Physics we have simple laws of gravity, motion, mass, thermodynamics and others that cannot or should not be violated. For example:

- For every action there is an equal and opposite reaction.
- A body in motion tends to stay in motion.
- The speed of light is constant.

In today's crazy world we have observed that many businesses seem to be making up their own rules, and some of them fly in the face of conventional business concepts. For example:

- Profits don't matter, only the number of eyeballs is important.
- We (the country) don't need to manufacture anything; we can become a service economy.
- You can sell your business for millions even if it has never made a profit.
- The conventional thinking that outsourcing is a great idea.
- I built this business for the customers (or the employees).
- I don't care about growth.
- The only way to improve my business is to get more sales.
- Someone should give me money for my business because it is a good idea.
- If I build it, they will come.

In the 1970's, I heard Rich Devos give a speech that he called Material Welfare, about the creation of wealth both Private wealth as well as National wealth. It changed my life. And if you are interested you can find it on YouTube. In that speech he said that:

MMW (man's material welfare) = NR (natural resources) + HE (human energy) x T (tools)

Meaning, if you give up any one of these things, or give up the control of one of these things, then you cannot create wealth. To be clear, there are a lot of businesses, where owners may get rich, that redistribute wealth without creating wealth, but even those businesses will eventually fail if they are not serving businesses that do create wealth.

Today I would like to offer some of my own laws of business:

- There are only two legitimate reasons to borrow money.
    - If that money can reduce expenses
    - If that money can increase revenues
- If you focus on net profit you won't need to chase cashflow.
- Both businesses, and economies have cycles, and you must be prepared for both the up and down cycles.
- It is better to end in pain than pain without end.
- It is not how much you make (sales); it is how much you keep (profit).
- Efficiency is not as important as throughput.
- If you treasure it, you should measure it.
- Control the tools, supplies, and the labor, or they will control you.
- Create a win-win, by understanding what is in it for the other guy.
- If you have to gamble, bet on the other person's "self-interest".
- Don't pay the ferryman until he gets you to the other side.
- Jesus may want you to feed the poor, but your banker wants you to make a profit first.
- Whenever possible, smooth out business fluctuation.
- Analyze and adjust, rinse and repeat.
- Always be humble and people will wish for your success.

- We always hear stories about those who gambled and won, but there are far more who gambled and lost.
- The last person in on any deal gets to set the rules.
- With enough volume you can almost produce it for free.

And my favorite:

- You can't be altruistic if you are out of business.

In some careers it is important to know Physics, but for a business owner it is critical to understand the Physics of Business.

- How knowing your breakeven point and contribution margin is important to setting your daily, weekly, or monthly goals.
- How the conversion equation is essential to good ROI on all your marketing.
- How to plan to get from where you are to where you want to be.
- How to negotiate with vendors and employees.
- How to add perceived value for your customers.
- How to pivot and take advantage as markets change.
- How to find the right employee for the right position.
- How to create Joint Ventures.
- How to expand your sales through upsell, down sell, and cross sell.
- How to survive a lack of resources and/or price wars.
- How prices are set by what you can afford to sell it for in combination with what the market will bear.
- How to plan for profit rather than HOPE it will be there at the end of the day.

It isn't enough to build a better mousetrap, it is essential to know where you are going, and how to get there without violating the Physics of Business.

How Much Profit Should I be Making? 8

One of the things that all people in business know is that all businesses, short of "not for profit" companies, is that profit is a primary objective. Although I could argue that even "not for profit" companies should be operating in a manner that should produce a profit, but that's a subject for a different time. That said, showing a profit is the goal if you have any ambition whatsoever of supporting your company's ongoing interest, and supporting you, the owner, over time. Profit defined is simply, "a financial gain, especially the difference between the amount earned and the amount spent in buying, operating, or producing something." But over the years and the thousands of business owners that I've asked this question, few could tell me how much profit they "should" be making. I would typically hear responses regarding "industry average" and historical realities of their own company. After they've given me their thoughts, they would typically ask me, "what should it be?". And now we circle back...

Let me state that I am NOT a proponent of gouging your customers with excessive pricing for the benefit of showing more profit. Profit at the expense of others using unethical pricing practices is not, in my opinion what a free-market enterprise is about. At the same time, I hear a business owner tell me that he was given advice from his accountant that he shouldn't show a profit, or too much profit lest he will end up paying more in taxes. I am not in advocate of this practice either. Can you imagine the logic of using some slick accounting practice to minimize profit over several years?! Suddenly the business owner either wants to secure a loan or even sell his business and the business appears to have not been profitable for years. Ooops... now what?

We may have stated this in other blogs or perhaps our Biz-easy Podcast but profit should be planned. It is not a, "wait until years' end and see what's left over" proposition. As you understand your cost of goods as a percentage of total revenues, or your gross margin, and have factored your fixed costs or overhead, you understand your breakeven. If your pricing policy is in alignment with these numbers, your planning for profit can then be established. I mentioned earlier that most business owners can usually quote industry averages. I imagine that this is a good place to start. It's always been my belief that average is simply the best of the worst, or the worst of the best. Does anyone strive to be average?

Your first assumption thereafter is to achieve better than average. But before you start raising prices, there is a multitude of other "variables" in the business to consider.

- Am I purchasing effectively?
- Am I turning my inventory properly?
- Are my labor efficiencies in check?
- Am I minimizing unnecessary overhead costs to the best of my ability?
- Have I done an effective "competitor" price comparison lately?
- Do I have a grasp on what the market will bear at this juncture?

Not to beat a dead horse with the over-use of an expression but, if you treasure it, you should measure it. If you have managed to answer all of these questions with an affirmative, you can then beat the average... the industry profit average that is. There are so many variables within your business that you are tasked with controlling that is seems the easiest way to manage it all is to, "wait until years' end and see what's left over." You don't have to be an accountant but having the tools and or personnel that work with you to manage the variables becomes essential. Let's face it, this simple cost can make the difference between managing for profit or waiting 'till the end.

We keep handy a list of most industries and their respective profit averages. Most of this information can be discovered with a deep dive on the internet but the more you dial down on your business, its specialties, uniqueness, and product/service mix, the more convoluted it becomes. Don't become discouraged. My humble advice is to figure out, with as much precision as you can, how much profit you have been making in recent months (and years) and prepare yourself a report. From this report you can look at seasonal or fluctuations that occur in your business on a yearly basis. As an example, I was working in the tuxedo business for over 15 years. The tuxedo industry is unique in that it caters to groups and individuals all whose demand occurred in about a 3-month span; weddings and proms. In that day, a vast majority of formal occasions occurred between April and June. Aside from a small demand spike in the fall, 80% of the revenues were generated in only 3 out of 12 months. Pricing policy and cashflow planning were absolutely essential to survive. Labor efficiencies and demand for labor in the busy months were additional challenges.

Not all businesses have the seasonal fluctuations that the tuxedo industry has but the tracking of costs does affect all industries. Knowing your profit history coordinated with your profit expectations will invariably compel you to plan more effectively. That is if profit is something you strive for, and I assume it is. To share another of my most prized expressions, "it's not how much you make, it's how much you keep!"

Adjusting Your Company Culture 9

Once upon a time, there was an empire that made many demands upon its institution. The candidate, to be included, had insistence placed upon timeliness, thoroughness, expedience, and abject attention. It believed that for an individual so worthy to join its assembly, abiding by a precise doctrine of behavior with a host of specifically outlined rules of conduct was paramount to inclusion. The empire governed with the adage, "The beatings won't stop until the morale improves!"

Okay, maybe this is a bit overstated. But this short missive described the relationship between the employer (the "empire"), and the employee (the "candidate"). It was not uncommon for an employer to feel that an employee should do a good job because they, "should be happy to have a job." And "your reward for your work is your paycheck." Any of these phrases sound familiar? My, have things changed. Welcome to the 21st century.

Over the course of generations, the relationship between an employer and employee have changed so significantly that the terms "Corporate Social Culture" and "Company Culture" are now part of our everyday lexicon AND an important part of our finding a new employer.

According to Indeed, a prominent search engine for employment placements, 46% of job seekers who considered a job but did not apply to it said they ultimately chose NOT to apply because they didn't feel it would be a good culture fit. Almost half of potential employees are willing to state that how they are treated at work will make the decision to apply, or not to apply. It forces us to ask ourselves, what does a good culture look like, and more critically, how do we determine if the one you are in currently meets the standard of a good culture.

We can all attest to knowing what a bad culture looks like. Visiting a restaurant, retail store or any business where employees are obviously unhappy speaks to a poor culture. From where does this stem? Over the years, the work duties, and responsibilities for most companies, aside from automation in most cases, hasn't really changed. However, the way employees, or "team members" as we now identify employees, HAS changed if a proper culture is to be achieved. Few people will accept being chastised by a supervisor in the presence of fellow employees or worse, in front of customers. I believe that this has become somewhat of a social norm. Taking it a step further, we must employ the Golden Rule: treating others as one wants to be treated.

Where does changing a company culture start? Having experienced a wide variety of situations where employees are unhappy, I will tell you without equivocation that changing a company culture starts at the top, the

Owner, President and/or CEO. From there, all levels of the organizational structure must participate in a change-management initiative to improve two things: **[1] Leadership**, with a keen sense of direction for the company and all its team members. And **[2] a communication network** that allows the dialog to flow to all members of the team. A leader's greatest achievement is a human and social one which stems from his understanding of his fellow workers and the relationship of their individual goals to the group goal that they must carry out. His ability to accomplish this is predicated on his ability to communicate, mostly through listening, to the individual to determine both.

It is no longer the pay status of a job alone or fear of retribution that motivates people to be at their best or do their best for the employer. Without over-simplifying, most people will accomplish more and perform better if they are happy and rewarded accordingly. It's not hard to agree that "happy employees are productive employees".

With the dynamic changes that have occurred in the employment landscape, more specifically in this century, people will do well at what they do if they feel appreciated for what they do and recognized for what they do.

Steve Jobs has been quoted as saying, "It doesn't make sense to hire smart people and then tell them what to do; we hire smart people so they can tell us what to do." A collaborative work environment where employees input and suggestions are solicited without judgment is a workplace where employees can improve, grow, and be appreciated. After all, gaining feedback from the person charged to perform a responsibility will logically yield the most valuable feedback – in theory, they do it all day long.

It has been uncharacteristic of management in the past to seek input from their staff and in so doing make them partners in the quest. Today, it becomes essential to make a habit of that process through the vehicles of regular performance review and a more integrated People Operations initiative. To quote another Titan of business, Sir Richard Branson of the Virgin cache of businesses, "A company's employees are its greatest asset, and your people are your product".

People today have access to more information at their fingertips than any other time in history. Effective leadership and an organization armed with this notion can realize that their own team members are a unique and useful resource for improvement and innovation. Collaboration of management and team benefits both and effectively accomplishes the reward/recognition component of a proper company culture.

As part of the new age of employee-employer relationships have evolved, a "work-life balance" has also become part of our dialog in team member satisfaction. Seeking out the "WIIFM" (what's in it for me) from your current staff and while adding additional staff members is a message all leadership must consider. As the only thing constant in the universe is change, we must adapt to new expectations to stay relevant and productive in business. Then again, you can always choose not to. But it will be at the peril of your business.

Shortage of Labor 10

Paul from California asks: How can I grow my business with a shortage of labor?

Great question Paul, and in my opinion the answer will be found by doing many things not just one thing.

Indeed, Business Owners across the country have been squeezed by the pandemic, by government regulations, lack of customers, lack of employees, increased wages, and increased costs.

Tony Robbins, amongst others, have said; "if you are not growing you are dying" ... Then how can we grow our businesses when the world seems like it is working against us?

Multi-prong Approach:

First, let us address rising costs of labor and materials. The short answer is "pay it and pass it on". But it isn't always easy to raise prices, is it? And some businesses have constraints regarding pricing that may already be locked in. But for those of you that have control of your pricing consider this; typically, when a business raises prices, without increased costs, by a mere 10%, it can afford to lose 30% of it's business without diminishing its bottom line. This would mean you could do what you do with roughly 30% less labor and remain as profitable with a simple, modest price increase. If your costs have gone (or will soon go) up, perhaps you could still sustain a 15-20% decrease in business without affecting the bottom line. (Please reach out if you want to understand the math better)

Second, we look at efficiency, or more importantly, "throughput". How can we improve the throughput (output) of the work that our company does? I won't go through the whole process of how to approach throughput improvement here, but if you are interested in learning more, please contact me directly. But imagine that we could just improve our output by 10%, that would probably mean you only need to recruit half as many people as you think you need now.

Third, we need to better retain the good workers that we have right now. Of course, moving people up the pay scale as quickly as they may deserve and bonus programs will help retain. But I would first look at the "culture" and working environment of your present operation. Is it a happy place or is it "toxic"? Find out why your best performers enjoy working here, ask yourself is there something you can do to make it more enjoyable. Just like "adding value" to your product or service, how can you add value to your workplace? Remember that wages are usually 3rd or 4th on the list of reasons that someone works for you. It is those intangibles that make work rewarding.

Forth, solve the recruitment problem! And here is why it is so important; imagine that in this difficult business atmosphere that you somehow had an unlimited supply of labor, and that your competitors continued to struggle with the labor shortage. It would be a tremendous competitive advantage, a time to grow, and take a bigger percentage of the available market share. It would set your business on a trajectory for exponential growth in the years/decades to come. Therefore, as difficult a task as solving this problem is, the value of solving is huge, and an opportunity that will only be here for a limited time.

The solution includes many of the things that you are already doing, but just like customer acquisition, employee acquisition is a "marketing problem". And when it comes to marketing the creation of a MDP (Market Dominating Position) or USP (Unique Selling Position) is the critical first step. Then using the same conversion equation to produce conversion, compelling offer, and most of the other marketing concepts that we teach to business owners daily will become the process to having both unlimited customers and applicants.

While it would be difficult to go into great details of these concepts within this response, I do hope this helps you Paul, and other business owners that struggle to solve the employment problem that face most business owners today. Please feel free to reach out if you would like more details or to take a look at your specific circumstances.

Working Backwards 11

As analytical as I am, it took me way too late into my career to discover that I should always be planning backwards. My hope is that you learn this tactic earlier rather than later in your business life.

If we establish a benchmark of where your business is today and then set a goal of where you would like/need to be at a point in the future, we can then establish the difference, or delta, between those two numbers.

Let's say that your business revenue is one million and you need it to be two million within two years, or two years from today. That means we need to develop a 24-month plan that can grow our revenues by one million dollars...right?

All too often, we open the doors to our business and work as hard as we can and let our business grow organically, at its own pace, if you will, this is a mistake that I made years ago, please learn from my mistakes rather than your own.

Growth needs a plan, and owners need to work to a plan to realize the business that they richly deserve, and have put their life savings and efforts into.

A farmer without a plan is a gardener. A farmer plans in order to maximize the yield of his/her crops, and so too must the business owner.

If we have a goal to add an additional one million to our top line revenue within 24 months then we best get started figuring out how we will accomplish that. Perhaps it is projecting out how many more units we need to sell each month, how many new customers we need each month, what additional products/services we can offer to our existing customers, or possibly a price increase.

If revenue is the goal, then there are only so many ways to achieve that:

- Higher prices
- More volume
- More frequency
- Additional Products/Services

If net profit is the goal, then you have some other options too:

- More efficiency
- Controlling the cost of labor
- Automation
- Minimizing overhead
- Better purchasing of raw materials
- And others

The answer usually a combination of your choices above, and once you have decided which vehicles to use to get you to your destination a route must be established.

- How much should I increase my prices?

- How can I improve my marketing to drive new customers to my door?
- How will I increase the frequency of purchases?
- What additional products or services are wanted by my customers?
- Where should I advertise?

Most of these questions, that answers are required for planning, will not be answered immediately, but will become apparent over time IF YOU stay focused. Getting distracted can derail your plan before it has had a chance to succeed.

So now you have decided (for example) that you need more customers. How many will you need to add each month for 24 months to get you to your goal. Map that out AND each month write how many you got. If you fall short this month you now know that you need to make up that shortfall next month. Keeping track each month is your early warning system which allows you to analyze and adjust.

When you are not hitting your targets more analysis is required. Ask yourself why. Do we need to adjust our marketing message? Do we need to audit to make sure everyone is asking "do you want fries with that?" Did we give our customers a reason to say yes to us over our competitors?

You are probably saying, "Skip, when you lay it out it is a simple concept. But I see it as overwhelming in practice."

And I say, "The simplification is so you can understand what needs to be done. But you are correct it can be a handful."

But here is why it is important; the big players in your market are out-planning you. They probably have dedicated people that do nothing but these planning, strategizing, and marketing. And your small competitors are not doing these things at all, thereby giving you a competitive advantage.

This is your opportunity to carve out your fair share of the market, to hold the big players back while eating the other competitor's lunch. If it were easy, you would have even more competitors.

What in the world is RIF? 12

We are all familiar with business expressions, platitudes and the ever-changing landscape business undergoes with a changing economy. Such is the case with management concepts and processes to deal with them. RIF is the acronym for "Reduction In Force". What's that, you say?! In the 80's the same concept was called "Down-Sizing" while in the 90's we called it "Right-Sizing". Sound more familiar? The process by which a company reduces its workforce to adapt to a decrease in human capital (personnel) needs is common when the company encounters a decrease in demand for that product or service in the market. So how and when does a company decide that a "RIF" is necessary? Let's discuss...

If you've followed contemporary business news, you have likely heard that Bed, Bath and Beyond has recently closed over 200 of its stores across the country. The reason that the retail chain made this move has not been widely debated but the outcome was in the cards as little as 2 years ago. At its peak, most stores employed 30 to 50 employees per location. As sales began to decline, the need for logistics personnel, sales staff and administrative people also declines. Similarly, Toys-R-Us and Radio Shack recognized their demise years ago largely for reasons of demand, available options, and an inability to change with the changing economy. As you would know, most of these types of declines happen gradually. Thus, personnel lay-offs and employment terminations also come gradually.

Then there is the tech and online industries who deliver a product that is not on the shelf and doesn't require great retail space or sales personnel like a Bed, Bath and Beyond store requires. The most of their staffing comes in the form or programmers, coders, marketing professionals, and host of other administrative personnel. In these cases, most of the employed persons are viewed on the income statement as "overhead", much like office rent and utilities. There are a variety of ways by which accounting and finance professionals measure and guide company performance and account for the human element. But the bottom line is, well in fact, the bottom line. If any company recognizes, hopefully in advance, a gradual decline in sales and subsequently their profit, changes must be made to keep the company in solvency – and in operation.

In some of these cases, the company recognizes that innovation and technological advances in delivering their product or service requires fewer people to provide the same sales volume to the consumer with a non-diminishing bottom line. Hence, a RIF is inevitable. When the human element reaches a point where the gross margin can no longer support the existing overhead with a planned profit outcome, changes are often made. It is never a comfortable event for a company but in the interest of its investors and its appeal in the marketplace to stay in business, a RIF may become its only option. In most such cases when insolvency or bankruptcy is the predicted outcome, it is understood that all other cost savings options are considered before the company chooses to reduce its workforce.

The unfortunate reality is that some company management teams may be operating with insufficient information (financial data) to accurately predict future outcomes. In other cases, an unsteady management team may ignore the signs of insolvency for entirely too long. In each case, it is not unusual for a CEO or Board Chairman to step in and make the hard decision. When the afore mentioned organizational decision-makers are faced with the choice, it is for the benefit of the rest of the staff and its investors, either shareholders or the creditors. But the outcome is required. The prevailing question becomes, "Is a RIF avoidable?" The answer is complicated, but the logic is simple.

A RIF is largely a process that a company of many employees must employ. But even a small business of 10 or fewer employees can recognize when they are slumping into a place of financial concern. The qualifier here is IF... If they can or choose to see through the window of financial measurables and make a decision that will alter the course of the company before it gets worse. Are they properly measuring company performance, product and sales performance, rising cost controls, gross margin, profit margin along with fluctuations in market demand and a host of other measurable KPI's (Key Performance Indicators). If they are truly on their game, the simple answer is often "yes", yes, they can make incremental changes to avoid having to make big changes.

It's a cautionary tale to see companies like Meta, Amazon, Zoom, E-Bay, PayPal, IBM and Spotify who have recently had to embrace a RIF for a failing to deliver the profit performance that is expected by its investors – stockholders. The smaller the company, the easier it is to control. That is IF you watch the KPI's. At the rate that multi-national companies generate revenue and must control the many moving parts required to stay competitive, it almost seems easy by comparison to control a much, much smaller company. My business colleague and friend, Skip often says, "If you treasure it, you should measure it!" For all of you reading this blog who own a small business or even work at a small to medium size company – understand how you (and others, particularly leadership) can measure your performance and that of the company to make correctional changes before they get worse. After all, Stephen Covey was quoted as saying, "I am NOT a product of my circumstances, I AM a product of my decisions."

Recession Proofing Your Business 13

When you turn on financial news everyone is speculating about the coming recession. I wish I was smart enough to predict with any certainty if, when, and how deep it will be, but I am not going out on that limb.

But I can say that preparedness is always a smart move! Any Business Owner that waits without making appropriate preparations are certainly playing with fire.

So how do you make your business ready for whatever the economy throws at us? Well, that is much easier said than done, but here we go with the punch list:

FIRST: Hoard Cash – Sounds simple but let's get more specific...

- Put off large purchases as long as you can. If the purchase was going to be "a nice to have" that would not improve sales or lower expenses, then this is obvious. If it was to increase output then consider that if things go south you won't need as much capacity anyway, so plan accordingly.

- Make your operation more efficient. Lean but not Mean, finding less laborious ways of accomplishing just as much.
- Better utilization of the human and fixed assets that you have. This will ultimately lead to better efficiency.
- Eliminate any overhead where you can. Shop insurance, eliminate subscriptions, trim overhead positions if you can, etc.
- Do not increase your Debt Load. HOWEVER, if you are on some type of payment plan for existing Debt DO NOT attempt to pay it down at this time, because you will still need to make payments through the recession. Just keep that cash in reserve.
- Renegotiate with Suppliers. They may want to secure your loyalty before hard times hit.
- Watch and collect your Accounts Receivable more aggressively.

Now these are things that are always important in business and should be done regularly. But the goal here is to make as large a stack of cash as we can in order to help us through the lean times ahead.

In an economy that cash is in shorter supply, you're having plenty of cash makes you king/queen.

SECOND: Secure Loyalty – Make sure your existing customers are happy.

- Reach out, follow up, and secure their loyalty.
- Create added value rather than lowering prices. This can be in delivering a better product or in providing better service.
- Create Loyalty Incentives.

- Look at your warranties. Perhaps there is a way to add value and reduce risk for the Customer.
- Perhaps, refer business to your customer(s) once and a while. This gains HUGE Loyalty. This is critical so that they stay with you through the leans times and your customer loss is way less than your competitors.

THIRD: Lower Your Personal Overhead – Every household requires different amounts of cash each month.

- Eliminate or reduce expenses where you are able. Subscriptions, utilities, retail purchases
- Pay down credit cards
- Pay off loans that are close to term

If you can reduce your monthly cash needs, the panic won't be as desperate if that time comes. And it will allow you to keep a little more cash in the business to provide even more safety as well as growth. If you don't do these things now, you may be forced to do them during the recession without nearly as much planning and positive results.

LASTLY - Taking Advantage of a Changing Economy

Let's assume that you have done these things successfully and have more than adequate cash reserves. Ask yourself "Do you want to come out alive, or in a stronger position after the recession?"

During a Recession is a great time to grow IF you have deep enough pockets. As you know people can make money in a Bear Market if they play their cards right.

Buying Up Your Competitors – There will be some great bargains available.

- Do not pull the trigger too soon on buying during a Recession. The later you wait the better the price AND the sooner to the end of the Recession which will preserve your cash.
- Buying Competitors will give a larger slice of the existing market now and especially after the Recession is over.

Expand to new locations – Landlords are looking for you.

- Whether you rent or buy that next location you should be able to negotiate better terms.
- Perhaps you can time that new location to open just as the Recession ends.
- It will be easier to find and negotiate with contractors while their business is slow.

Now Make that Large Purchase – Again, their business is probably slow.

- Time is good to negotiate better pricing or financing.

Don't Wait for the Rush – When the Recession is Over it is Too Late.

- Hire Employees
- Stock up on supplies
- Don't wait for your competitors to start the ball rolling again.

Everything I have talked about today depends on how deep your pockets are and how much cash you have hoarded, not to mention timing. A few sacrifices today could mean you end up with twice as much (or more) business after the sun comes back out.

So be wise, be fruitful, and be careful...

Selling 14

It has always been my contention that "people don't like to be sold, but they do like to buy". I had adopted this notion long ago when I was in the tuxedo industry. I was responsible for recruiting, hiring, and training sales and management personnel for a 130-store retail operation in the Midwest. I have had the good fortune of working with many exceedingly qualified salespeople, many of whom had very little background or experience in selling a product or service to the consumer. I have recognized there are a few key components of people who are well suited to be the representative of the product for a service to the customer. As a qualifier, let me say that I, in no way, see myself as an expert in sales. But I position myself as a person who CAN see when a person has made a significant connection between a product and/ or service and a customer's need. Moreover, I have seen when a representative has made an efficient conversion to a customer's need, to a customer's want, and that is the essence of selling in my humble opinion.

We've all had a memorable, albeit laughable experience of being sold to. I defer to a recent phone call from a person who called me to offer me an "affordable" repair warranty for a car I no longer owned. How about a "better" internet connectivity in my home only to find out that they didn't offer service in my area. On the flip side, I think we can all attest to knowing someone who can, "sell ice to Eskimos". Can I even say that anymore? Never-the-less, we know a person who has sold us something that perhaps we didn't even know we needed until we heard the "pitch". I believe that there is a certain attitude, if you will, or skill in being able to communicate the value of a product to a person they never met. So, what is it do you suppose? I also know many who are true targets for aggressive, and even non-aggressive salespeople. Perhaps they just can't say "no", but they end up buying everything offered, until one day they just avoid the situation altogether.

My simple credo in doing business with others is this... **Know, like, trust.** I believe that you must first know someone, before you can decide if you like them, to then conclude that you can trust them. Maybe I'm not Will Rogers who was quoted as saying, "I never met a man that I didn't like". But my thought process follows a simple pattern. It's a process that I share often when talking to others in business about their marketing, advertising and even networking efforts. When you are in a situation where it's a brief encounter, a chance meeting or even if you are in pursuit of a product or service, what makes the difference for you to engage or not to engage? I for one, think it is in fact about attitude. It's also about presentation. I'm not sure anyone is comfortable being cornered. I also don't respond well to a hard come-on. But perhaps I'm a bit too analytical to be a fair judge.

As I mentioned earlier, I pride myself in being able to see a connection between a person selling and a person buying. It happens when the person presenting has recognized a need, a solution or an answer to the person being presented to. Further, they do so in a manner that is not over-bearing or intrusive. I have always been a strong proponent of conveying benefit and value to fulfill a relationship between a buyer and a seller. That sounds pretty simple and straightforward but how do you suppose you get to knowing "what the customer wants"? Answer: You ask questions. Assumptive lead-ins are dangerous. Before I get too much further, I must interject that before you can make any inroads with a prospective client/customer/consumer, you must be passionate about what it is you are presenting. If YOU don't believe in it, why should anyone else? Fair, yes?!

Passion and attitude are key. Are they quantifiable? That is a great argument, but I believe everyone has a sense that they are being sold when those 2 qualities are not present. I also believe that most, if not all buying decisions are made with emotion, but they only hold when they are supported by reason and logic. Sure, I'd like to spend all of my free time in the tropics sipping a Mai Tai but logic tells me that it's not practical, reasonable or logical. However, if I can reasonably justify the cost with the product for it's return AND I get to sip a Mai Tai now and again, then let's get busy. No, I have never purchased a time share but you get the analogy. The attitude of the presenter comes into play when he/she doesn't over-step their limitations for presentation. Embellishing return, avoiding small print and worst of all, misrepresentation are all deal killers. A person will believe most of what they hear until they hear something that they absolutely do NOT believe, then the rest is up for question.

Converting a need to a want, that is the true deal maker. I trust most people to know what they need, but I absolutely trust someone to know what they want. If the need is easily converted to a want and vice versa, you are going in the right direction. That's the value and benefit part. Nobody buys a self-propelled lawn mower because it's more efficient but because it provides a benefit over one that is not self-propelled. It's easier, but it's not more efficient. That's a benefit. Will I spend the extra $100 for the self-propelled mower? If I want that benefit, yes. Do I need that benefit? Not really. I failed to mention that before you can present a product or service to a prospective customer, you'd better know what you're talking about. Learn it, understand it, and be an expert or you're going to be on an uphill battle. If your passion for the product still holds – you're almost there.

Selling is not for everyone. I once heard that, "We don't see things as they are, we see things as we are." Your perspective on the product or service is based on how YOU see it. Learn how to see it as THEY see it. If how you see it and how they see it are alike, then you are well on your way to making a great connection. Because if YOU think it's too expensive, you'll convey that in your attitude and your presentation. If my diagnosis of selling style seems a bit esoteric, so be it. Maybe that's why sales people sometimes get a bad rap. I'll repeat my opening contention... "People don't like to be sold, but they do like to buy!"

Ideas are Easy, Implementation is Hard 15

You probably have a great idea for a business. Perhaps it comes from a hobby or interest that you have, or people have told you that they love your brownies or your handyman skills.

The truth is that most everyone has "an Idea" a few times a year, but what happens next is critical.

Without historical data for your specific idea these early months of planning become wrought with delusional pitfalls. What I mean by that is it is very easy to lie to yourself and not even know it. Here are a couple of examples:

- A well-meaning friend or relative tells you your crazy and it will never work, and you believe them.

- A well-meaning friend or relative tells you it's a great idea, and you believe them.

- You are already selling to a few customers from your part-time, home based, hobby business, so you tell yourself that there must be a huge market for what you sell.
- When projecting how many units a day you will sell once open.
- Not considering all the overhead, the cost of goods, and whether the price you can charge will sustain all those expenses.
- In determining what size the business should be.

These are just a few examples, but there are many more. The reason it is so easy to lie to yourself is the lack of data. You might have access to similar businesses' numbers, but those numbers may or may not apply to your cost, especially because for you to build a similar business will cost a lot more in today's dollars.

So, if we do not have sufficient data with which to base decisions on, how do we "project" what your business will, [1] Cost to start, [2] Cost to run, [3] Must sell each day.

Feasibility Analysis is the answer. And when it comes to Feasibility, I have a few things to say, as I have been doing them for 30 years, and I have a BIG issue with the way most feasibility is done, so please bear with me and see if my method makes sense.

Conventional "proforma" Feasibility Analysis is done in a Profit & Loss format. Line by line you will enter your monthly fixed expenses, take a guess at your monthly sales revenue, and work your cost-of-goods expenses as a simple percentage of revenue...DONE.

When I look at these types of projections all I see is 20-30 lines of data that we likely lied to ourselves when entering, and one line, the revenue, that is purely a S.W.A.G. (scientific wild a** guess). Your Banker knows this and therefore disbelieves everything you've projected.

The best way to combat against is what I like to call a "bottom-up" approach, rather than the "top-down" method previously explained.

When we look at construction on a per square foot basis, when we look at sales as units, labor as hours, and commissions on dollars, determine how much labor and supplies will go into each unit sold, we can begin to get a good idea of what the optimum size should be, how many employees we will need, how many hours a week we will need to be open, what the price needs to be and/or how many units need to be sold each day. Then we can ask ourselves; can we sell that many units a day, can we find that many employees at that wage, how many hours a day should we be open... are these expectations reasonable?

By using the "what if" method we will be able to optimize the size and scope of the operation and adjust pricing and volume until we have dialed in the correct configuration that will maximize profitability and more importantly the chances for success.

The size of your business is very critical component. It is just as big a faux pas to build it too small as it is to build it too big, and this method will allow you to find the size that is "just right". Therefore, I recommend going through this process before you determine location and real estate.

Thirty years ago, when I first started doing Feasibility, I was only able to tell if a business was viable or not, and I saved a lot of people from making a huge mistake. But today when I perform this service for potential businesses, I am able help them understand the variables, the reasons why the business model won't work, and help the tweak the business model for success.

You, the business owner have a vision, you know what you would like to do, but may need expert assistance putting the numbers and the data together so that you can find funding and to help but shape that vision into a model that has the greatest chance for success.

If you're good at numbers you can use this method too, but here is why it is best to have a third-party work with you: A neutral party can help you to not exaggerate your numbers, and they will add credibility to your business plan for Lenders to better believe your projections. And when using the "Bottom-up" method the Lender can see the rationale used in projecting those numbers.

How to Write a Business Plan 16

In the old days when you wrote a Business Plan the shear volume of it was important to plunk down on a Banker's desk. It showed that you have thought through many of the details and showed due diligence.

Today however brevity is appreciated. The reader wants to get right to the heart of the matter; what are you looking to do, how much can it make, how are you going to capture the market, and who are the key people involved. Regardless of the order you provide this information this is probably the order they will read it.

Officially, the components of a full-blown Business Plan are as follows:

Executive Summary

The first and most important section, summarizing everything you hope to accomplish with your business.

Company Legal Description

Defines your company's legal status.

Products and Services

Lays out the products and/or services you plan to offer to customers and clients.

Marketing Plan

Explains your plan for reaching, acquiring, and retaining customers for your business.

Operations Plan

Shows that you've thought through the logistics of actually operating your company, including hiring staff, shipping, storage, and more.

Organization and Management

The organizational structure of your company — what does staffing look like? Who manages which teams?

Bios of Key Management

Highlights the experience and competence of the key leaders in your company.

Personnel Plan

A deeper dive into your plan for hiring and retaining the best staff to manage and run your company.

Intellectual Property and other Key Assets

What are the key assets your company has ownership of? Even if it's just an idea that you have legal claim to, list it here.

Financial Plan

Lays out the cost of everything mentioned in the previous sections, plus your plan for funding to cover those costs.

Appendix

Nitty gritty details that you can reference in other sections of your plan. This will include tables, charts, budgets, and other "hard" figures.

However today we will focus on the four important parts previously mentioned, and keep in mind, what they call the One-Page Business Plan, while an exaggeration of how short it should be, is becoming more and more popular. Therefore, if you focus on these four parts and add others as desired, then you should be fine for any lender or investor.

Executive Summary

The Executive Summary is right at the front of the document and the first thing the reader sees. In this section we want to educate the reader.

- What will the business will be selling.
- Why you are different from your competitors.
- How you will capture your share of the marketplace.
- The size and scope of the business.
- How much capital you are looking for.
- What is in this for the lender or investor.

Try to avoid the personal stories and history of how and why you found yourself wanting to open this business. Instead try to engage the reader, educate them about this business, and then tell them what is in it for them.

Financial Plan

Although the Financial Plan is usually found towards the end of this document it will most likely be the next section the reader flips to, so spend some time to make them easy to read, comprehensive, and compelling.

Referring to the previous chapter, I recommend doing a complete Feasibility Analysis BEFORE writing a business plan, using variables that allow you to dial in the optimal business model, size, offering, pricing, etc.

From that Feasibility Study you will pull from it; a Proforma first year month-by-month P&L, a 3/5-year Proforma P&L, a Break-Even Analysis, Itemized list for Cost of Startup, Cash Flow analysis, and Contribution Margin Analysis (or something that shows just how profitable you will be) for inclusion into the business plan.

Keep in mind you want to be conservative in your projections, but NOT TOO conservative, as your reader will probably discount your numbers.

Marketing Plan

If we have done our work properly the reader will be saying to themselves "wow, that looks profitable. But I wonder how they are going to get all those sales!", so this is usually the next section they will read.

Providing marketing demographics can be useful in showing just how little of the population you need to sell to in order to reach your numbers BUT MORE IMPORTANTLY you want to show them:

- Why your offering will be more enticing to the buyer.
- What makes you special in the marketplace.
- How do you plan to reach those buyers.
- What your message to those buyers will be.

Do not be afraid to be specific and detailed as to your plans to reach and sell your market. Many prospective Business Owners have a "if I build it, they will come" mentality, and this thinking is deadly, even with a great location or product.

If there is anyplace in the Business Plan that you need to show you know what you are talking about, this is the place. This is the place that proves you have something MORE than just a good idea.

Bios of Key Management

Also located toward the back of the document, and while it would be tempting to simply paste everyone's resume in this section, I would advise that you do some serious editing and boil each persons experience down to the things that make them well suited for THIS business.

I have done several Business Plans with only these four components, I've also seen them about as small as this article, however sprinkling in other sections as needed and a few pages longer is more common.

Also, do not underestimate the power of artwork that shows your products, location, etc., as well as charts and graphs that depict your financials.

Working ON your Business vs. IN Your Business 17

To the casual reader, this title might seem a bit odd. To anyone who has been involved in services provided to small and medium size business owners, this concept is quite clear. Moreover, the concept is critical for a business owner to understand his/her most significant role in their own business. For clarification, you may have heard the title "Owner/Operator" when identifying a small business owner. This simply means that he/she not only owns the business but is the person responsible for performing the work. Best example: Gus's Landscape Service – where Gus owns the business AND does all the grass cutting himself. Business ownership most always starts here.

As business owners grow their business they will diversify, segregate and delegate various responsibilities within the structure of the work performance. When Gus decides that he has more work than he can handle, he hires his son Buster whereafter they both are doing the work. As business grows even further with more landscape jobs, Buster's friend Billy joins the team. Skipping forward, Gus has 20 employees now, all out in the field with 4 trucks, trailers, and equipment while Gus's wife Glenda is at home dutifully billing customers, preparing paychecks and paying bills. Once a business owner like Gus manages his business to hit roughly about a $1M revenue mark (most often less), Glenda realizes that the company is making more money each month, but, to her and Gus' surprise, they are keeping less. Sure, Gus isn't working the long hours he used to but there is less money in the bank, less money to pay bills, less money to pay for repairs and less money in their pocket as the owners of the business. What happened? How is that possible? What now?

This quick missive is a description of the typical progression of a small business owner. At this point a decision must be made. In my experience, the business owner who has NOT recognized the relationship between "working IN" the business versus "working ON" the business, he will typically decide to dial it back. He'll reduce his staff, sell off a truck, trailer or two and jump back in the truck and work more hours because he was making more money when "he was doing more work". Not surprisingly, a business owner may find himself in this exact same situation 2 and 3 times in his career. "High volume – low income" activity to "low volume – high income" activity, without realizing that he, yes Gus the owner, is the instigator of this reoccurring paradox. Unfortunately, by the time that Gus has come to this realization, he is now in his 50's and doesn't have the physical wherewithal to work long hours anymore. Gus never took the time to learn the value of "systems" dependency", versus "people" dependency – his current situation. More accurately, we can now circle back to Gus working IN the business versus ON his business.

Anyone in the business advisory industry who has had the good fortune of meeting a business owner like Gus and who understands the simple concept of "ON" vs "IN", would be delighted to walk Gus through a series of questions that would bring enlightenment to his situation. The most fundamental tenets of business operation are all absent when this situation occurs, and the remedy can make the most remarkable changes toward success when they are understood and implemented. For example;

- How do you track employee productivity?
- How do you schedule your workflow for optimal use of travel time and equipment?
- How do you price your service as to be competitive and still cover costs?
- Does your pricing cover your overhead burden?
- Are you managing cashflow effectively to purchase equipment as needed?
- Does your staff have the same objectives for performance as you do?
- What is the compelling offer that you have that makes you a better choice for a client?
- How do you measure all these cost variables in real time?
- How much money SHOULD you be making?

I would argue that if Gus' company is making more and keeping less, he likely would not be able to answer these questions with any credibility. He knows what he knows because he has been doing the work for years, many years. He taught his son and his staff how to do a good (maybe even great) job, but it still comes back to the most important question; who is managing the business? The concept, when broken down in this manner seems easy enough, but when you're on the inside looking out, it's too easy to get crowded with the forest that the trees seem out of focus.

Running a business without a fundamental concept of measuring workflow process, managing people for performance with cost controls and measuring all cash in and cash out transactions without having a specific expectation for outcome can be daunting. What's that old expression, "If you don't know where you're going, any road will get you there". This blog isn't designed to examine all the ins and outs of working ON the business but rather to be an identification of what happens when there is no distinction. Working IN the business may make an owner feel all warm and fuzzy while he delights his customers, but if there is any inclination to make money so that he can grow, engage the help of others and enlarge his reach while being able to support his family and ultimately retire... well, only HE can decide if it's worth it to make the important change in his role. Becoming a businessman instead of simply a business owner is a decision that each person who endeavors into working for himself must make. Should he NOT make the decision, the outcome will invariably be the same – the owner will be managed by the business rather than the business managed by the owner.

Articulation 18

I recently saw a post on Facebook; "I couldn't love him anymore". I wondered if that meant their love affair was over, or, quite the opposite, that she was at the maximum amount of love.

All too often we think others understand just what we mean when we direct our employees, when we are speaking with our boss, the board of directors, or most importantly with our customers. It is always clear in our mind what message we are trying to convey but it seems that what is understood can often be significantly different. While thinking about this notion, how often do you suppose this occurs?

"I know you think you understand what you thought I said but I'm not sure you realize that what you heard is not what I meant."

When I am creating a spreadsheet, a business plan, or discussing an issue with a business owner having troubles, I often say "if you can articulate it, I can build it, write it, or solve it". But sometimes I am led down a rabbit hole, thinking that they want something different than what they really need. Ideas are a wonderful thing, but without exactness in our communications those ideas will never come to fruition. Furthermore, in business it is equally important in our marketing message to our customers.

If you could know how much time was being wasted and accomplishments not realized in your business due to inarticulate instructions or communications, I think you would be surprised, and ready to do something about it.

The English language is NOT like numbers which are hard to misinterpret. It is wrought with ambiguity, but there are some things we can do about it.

1. Try to be exact in your instructions (or promises) to others.
2. When receiving instructions ask follow up questions for further clarity.
3. Make sure others are comfortable, and encourage them, to ask YOU follow up questions for clarity.
4. Use written communication whenever something is the least bit important.
5. Share your vision, goals, and the objectives, so that others understand what you are trying to accomplish, not simply what you want them to do.
6. Ask the listener questions to make sure they understand what you need/want.

In today's world of remote work, we tend to assign tasks or projects and walk away without much supervision, and all too often we are disappointed with the results. I would submit to you, that the answer is less about supervision and more about communication. It has been my experience that a lack of effective communication is the root cause of many of the issues and problems we encounter in business operations and in working with others, business or not.

One of the most common complaints about managers from their staff is this; "They are always setting me up for failure". To which I usually reply, "Any manager that actually sets someone up for failure is either foolish or inarticulate". Why? Because it is not in any manager's best interest to set another person up for failure, and therefore it is usually because of a lack of effective communications skills. This makes it difficult for them to make the manager look good by getting the job done professionally, efficiently, and/or to the customer's satisfaction.

We must use this imperfect language to convey the most precise instructions at all times. We can not be in such a hurry that we leave ambiguity in the mind of the listener, or not allow them to ask clarifying questions, else the instructor, as well as the instructed will be frustrated, never realizing their objectives.

Over time, as two people work together, they usually develop a shorthand, but we can never assume that the listener fully understands both the instructions as well as the objective. As you become more exact in what you ask for, it is then incumbent for the instructed to provide more exact projections, timelines, and efficiency. Compounding this, ambiguity breeds rework and waste. This recalls a quote we've all heard many times before; "Never enough time to do it right... but always enough time to do it over!"

When we talk about "communication skills" we often think about the humanity of when to talk, and how to talk to others, sensitivity if you will, so that we do not offend or become inappropriate. That's all well and good, but exactness in communication is far more important. Even in writing this short blog several edits were made in order to provide more clarity. Unfortunately, we don't have the luxury of rewriting our verbal communications over and over, so we must take other precautions and learn to be precise. Nothing will cause more angst and disappointment from two parties than ineffective communication.

Without exactness in our communications, we simply spin our wheels in the mud of ambiguity.

Business Valuation 19

It's not straightforward to define "business value". If you ask different business managers, they all have their respective answers when it comes to business value. So, what is a business valuation exactly. Business Value refers to the benefits a business generates for its stakeholders. Aside from the sale of your business there may be a few other times in your business life that you need to put a fair market value to your business. Here are a few of the reasons why you may need a Business Valuation:

1. When looking to sell your business
2. When looking to merge or acquire another company
3. When looking for business financing or investors
4. When establishing partner ownership percentages
5. When adding shareholders
6. For divorce proceedings

7. For dissolution of a Business Partnership

8. For certain tax purposes

9. For bragging rights... (Just kidding)

There are a large handful of ways to perform a Business Valuation, although several are more about determining the value of a publicly traded stock share. So today we will focus on a few methods used for most small and medium size businesses for one or more of the purposes previously stated.

In all methods there is a certain amount of subjectivity. The methods themselves are straight forward but the subjectivity comes into play when determining "future potential" also called "blue sky". This becomes the battlefield of the buyer and seller, as value is ultimately determined by the beholder.

Market Value Valuation Method

The Market Value method compares your business to similar businesses in your area that have sold. Almost exactly how residential real estate is valued, but with a much smaller sample size.

I cannot recommend this method because even though the size, and gross revenue may roughly match, profitability rarely does. Some business owners can squeeze more juice out their fruit than others. Also, locations are not equal and for a variety of other reasons it is difficult to get an apples-to-apples comparison with any other business.

I was recently involved with valuing a franchise operation where all the stores in the franchise were the same footprint. Even in this case, their profitability on roughly the same volume of business ranged from 10% of revenue to 38% of revenue. If the price for each were the same based on "Market Value", which store would you prefer to buy?

This being said, because this small business valuation method is relatively imprecise, your business's worth will ultimately be based on negotiation, especially if you're selling your business or seeking an investor.

Nevertheless, this valuation method is a good preliminary approach to gain an understanding of what your business might be worth, but you'll likely want to bring another, more calculated approach to the negotiation table.

Asset-Based Valuation Method

Asset-Based method is fairly straight forward. As the name suggests, you look at your balance sheet and subtract Liabilities from Assets and the remainder is the value of the business.

This method fails to take future potential into the equation, and is therefore a method to use when the business makes little or no profit each year or for the purpose of liquidation.

It can be a good valuation to do along side the method we are about to discuss, as sometimes a business is asset rich even at a depreciated value and if the value is close to the number of the next method it is easier to justify to the buyer because it is less subjective. Other times, this number might be considered the floor value of the business, or the least what the business should be worth.

Capitalization of Earnings Valuation Method

Capitalization of Earnings method, often called Cap Value, uses a method of future potential as its main driver.

In order to determine the Cap Value, one must first calculate the EBITDA, which is the annual earnings BEFORE Interest, Taxes, Depreciation, and Amortization.

EBITDA is the net profit a new owner could expect to earn if they simply maintain what you are doing presently. It strips away the "funny money" from the equation like depreciation and amortization which are not hard expenses, and because their tax rate and interest rates may be different than yours it removes them as well.

Once the EBITDA is determined we apply a Cap Rate multiplier. The multiplier is stated as a percentage, for example a 25% Cap Rate is a 4X multiplier because 25 goes into 100 four times. Therefore, the higher the percentage the lower the multiplier (i.e., a 50% Cap Rate would be a 2X multiplier). Don't worry to much about fractional math here, as most negotiations we talk about the multiplier not the Cap Rate.

There are two main subjective areas when doing this calculation or more precisely during the negotiation between the seller and buyer.

    1. What the multiplier should be

    2. The time period used in determining the EBITDA

Let's address these by looking at both the Buyer's and Seller's perspective.

Buyer's Point of View

When it comes to what multiplier should be used, let's look at this from the buyer's point of view. If they have the money to invest in your business, could they get a better rate of return in a safe, relatively risk-free investment. This is what Your Business is being compared against.

If they could double their investment in another place in 5 years, then why would they take the risk, responsibility, and work to give you 5 times EBITDA which equates to the same earnings? They will be measuring risk and profit based on what YOU did with the business not on what improvements they think they can bring to the table.

If you have a business that has a lot of real estate, like a hotel/motel or a farm, this automatically reduces much of the risk or value or equity and those businesses then usually deserve higher multipliers as people are usually more patient about the return on their investment. Conversely if you rent a location and have limited assets, then there is no fallback equity and those businesses have much smaller multipliers.

Each industry has a range of multipliers that work financially for those types of business, so I won't get into typical multipliers in this article, suffice to say those multipliers must work for the buyer.

There can be mitigating factors however that might make a buyer willing to pay more than calculated value such as changing landscape of the area, elimination of competition, changing demand, a strategic reason, or even changing technology.

Seller's Point of View

The Seller has put in a lot of work on building the business and perhaps experienced a recent downswing or upswing in both revenue and profit. He or she might want to get paid for recent growth by prorating the last 3 months to 12 months rather than the last 12 moths of financial history. Or if experiencing a downswing they might prefer to average the last 3 years of history to determine EBITDA. If you want to play this game, you had best be prepared to convince the Buyer as to why you think this is the fair way to value the business.

At the end of the day, this business is NOT worth what you say or calculate, it is worth what someone is willing to pay for it. If that is not enough, a Business Owner must be prepared to continue to make their money over time rather than through the sale of their business.

Modes of Persuasion 20

Aristotle coined the Greek terms "Ethos, Pathos, and Logos" to explain both the proof of artistic value and the modes of persuasion.

In business, as in life, persuasion is meaningful and important to every exchange with clients/customers and of course people. Presentations in business, especially in marketing, the delivery is meant to be a means to convey information that will help the audience make an informed decision about something, be it the how or why something is meaningful or necessary to another person or persons. I find it fascinating to tie both art and persuasion together but want to focus on the persuasion part of the equation. In homage to Aristotle let's call this "The Art of Persuasion" and break it down the way that he would.

Ethos

Ethos or the ethical appeal, means to convince an audience of the speaker's credibility and character.

The speaker would use ethos to show their audience that they are a credible source and is worth listening to. Ethos is the Greek word for "character." The word "ethic" is derived from ethos. Ethos can be developed by making yourself sound fair or unbiased, introducing your expertise, accomplishments, or pedigree, and by using correct grammar and syntax.

When I think about ethos, I like to emphasize empathy. When trying to convince someone to do something, never recommend something that is not in THEIR best interest. Even if that means losing the sale today, it sets you up for a long-term fruitful relationship, because you have gained a huge amount of trust.

Honesty gains trust, and trust gains sales.

Pathos

Pathos or the emotional appeal, means to persuade an audience by appealing to their emotions.

Authors use pathos to invoke sympathy from an audience; to make the audience feel what the author wants them to feel. A common use of pathos would be to draw sympathy from an audience. Another use of pathos would be to inspire anger from an audience, perhaps in order to prompt action. Pathos is the Greek word for both "suffering" and "experience." The words empathy and pathetic are derived from pathos. Pathos can be developed by using meaningful language, emotional tone, emotion evoking examples, stories of emotional events, and implied meanings.

You see this everyday in commercials using children, puppies, or other things that tug at the heart strings. They may be selling jeans or coffee, but the commercial barely mentions their product and rather seeks to evoke an emotional response.

Emotion gains interest, and interest gains sales.

Logos

Logos or the appeal to logic, means to convince an audience by use of logic or reason.

To use logos would be to cite facts and statistics, historical and literal analogies, and citing certain authorities on a subject. Logos is the Greek word for "word," however the true definition goes beyond that, and can be most closely described as "the word or that by which the inward thought is expressed" and "the inward thought itself". The word "logic" is derived from logos.

Logos can be developed by using advanced, theoretical, or abstract language, citing facts (very important), using historical and literal analogies, and by constructing logical arguments. People are seldom sold by use of logic, but logic is used to seal the deal. Using logic in your sales communications is designed to reduce "buyer's remorse".

Logic creates reasons, and reasons gain sales.

Conclusion

This subject matter is in play, and has been most of your life, to request, convince or simply convey an idea important to you to another person or persons. In business, especially in our marketing efforts we must make our greatest point often with the least number of words and phrases. To persuade your audience effectively, proper use of Ethos, Pathos, and Logos, once understood, becomes critically necessary. In our marketing efforts, we often refer to the conversion equation which describes the 4 parts of great marketing materials. For review they are as follow:

1. Interrupt
2. Engage
3. Educate
4. Offer

Typically, one might use Pathos in writing the Interrupt and Engage portions. The Educate might also contains Pathos, but should primarily contain Ethos and Logos.

When writing the **Interrupt** portion, we should be asking ourselves what problem my customer has that they wish they didn't. (Pathos)

When writing the **Engage** portion, we should illustrate what their life might be like if they didn't have the problem (also Pathos).

When writing the **Educate** portion, we should talk with authority how your company is best suited to fix that problem and exactly what you will do to solve the issue (Ethos and Logos).

And when writing the **Offer**, we want to make them an offer of which they would be foolish for not taking advantage (Ethos, Pathos, and Logos).

Who knew the scholars and Greek philosophers had prepared our marketing formulas and delivery methodologies hundreds, if not thousands of years ago? So, when you are developing marketing materials, or trying to convince someone to do something, don't reinvent the wheel - remember Aristotle; speak with authority, use passion and empathy, and then follow up with logic.

Need Money for Your Business? **21**

Every small to medium sized business owner at some point in time in their career has been asked this simple question. Whether it be from a credible finance company, a friend, a relative, an angel investor, a retail company, car dealer or a credit card company. The intrigue of the question evokes a whirlwind of thoughts, most of which revolve around the idea of how nice it would be to get an infusion of cash in their business. The answer to the question is generally the same but those who have been down the path of "getting money from a lender" realize it comes with a host of concerns and questions. I would submit to you that those who can demonstrate and/or prove that they can do well without it or simply don't need it will likely be the same people who are most likely to get it without a great degree of obstacles. Why is this so? The lender wants to be sure they will get their money back, albeit with the interest attached, but that the risk in making the loan is with as little risk to the lender as possible.

That said, most entrepreneurs need an infusion of cash at some point in time. The most common and obvious reasons are simple:

- Starting the business
- Expanding the business operations
- Buying new or innovative equipment
- Enlarging inventory
- Adding staff or sales personnel

The problem is that the more common reasons that entrepreneurs think they NEED money is for less enviable reasons:

- Can't make payroll.
- Can't sustain the accounts payable in a timely fashion.
- Not collecting receivables in a timely manner.
- An unexpected, unplanned major expense arises.
- The business owner hasn't kept up with his personal obligations and needs money.

The fact of the matter is the business owner hasn't managed his cash flow effectively often because their company has not been managed as profitably as it should be. As I traveled around the country visiting business owners, I would submit that 99 out of 100 business owners that I met with stated that "not adequate cash flow" was in the top 3 of their business challenges. To translate, "not adequate cash flow" really means that they need a cash infusion. My response to their challenge, always in the form of a question was, "what do you need the money for?" Invariably once we dialed in on the business's other challenges, it came down to the second set of reasons previously stated. Okay, so here we are, cash outflows exceed cash inflows. Let's dive deeper.

Whether you need money for start-up, expansion, enlarging equipment or inventory, or even to sustain business operations, the burden is on the borrower to demonstrate to a lender that there is little risk in lending the money. A lender never wants to think that you are borrowing money to pay off debt although there are many such companies that offer this option but at a substantial expense to the borrower. I learned early in my career using an excavation metaphor, "when you are in a hole and you want to get out, stop digging!" That said, getting a loan by showing the lender low risk can be challenging. A home loan or a car loan are quite common, and most people have managed through that circumstance before and generally with ease. The difference here is that the car or the house is collateral. In other words, the borrower decides to stop making payments and the lender takes back the car or the house. In a business, particularly one where the equipment or machinery will not satisfy the loan as collateral, the borrower must now prove that using the money from the loan, business operations and the profit thereby achieved will be able to make the loan payments. Put simply, they can't (or certainly don't want to) take the business away from you. For clarification, all SBA loans are determined this way.

Where to start... There are two things required by all lenders for business loans:

1. A Financial Report to "show how the money flows in and out of the company".
2. Business Plan to explain "how this business makes money so effectively".

On step one, the business must figure out exactly how much money you have coming in (cash inflows) and exactly how much money you have going out (cash outflows) and the schedule of each. This is a fundamental need. In the case of a start-up, the process is the same except the inflows and outflows will all be projections based on similar business models. Thereafter, determining how much money the investment will enhance the value or profitability of the company is key. In other words, you borrow to gain a return on investment (ROI). If you understand the fundamentals of an Income Statement and a Balance Sheet, you will notice that loan payments do not appear on the Income Statement, only the interest (an accounting lesson for another day). Thus, the operating profit of the company must exceed the debt service (loan payments) to determine that a loan is feasible. And THIS is how you can demonstrate that the risk to the borrower is minimal.

Once you've understood and substantiate the feasibility of someone loaning the company money from a cash flow perspective, get busy writing a plan. Start-ups write Business Plans explaining the nature of the business and how their particular business is uniquely positioned in the market to return to the owner more money than it takes to run it. The fundamentals of the report are concise but descript enough to make the lender realize how little risk there is in making the loan. Business Plan preparation has evolved over the years trending more toward an executive summary format with key unique, yet actual features that make the business low risk. Unfortunately, gone are the days of selling a lender into giving a loan based on flowery, compelling language, unrealistic blue-sky expectations and because it's your neighborhood banker.

In other words, do the due diligence required, provide the financial reality of the circumstance, then most of the other challenges of getting a loan will fall into place.

I appreciate that preparing yourself for a loan can sound dauting. I can assure you that it is dauting if you can't prove to yourself that if the roles were reversed, would you lend you the money? Referencing the many business owners that I've met with that said they didn't have "adequate cash flow", once they realized that their inflows wasn't the problem and instead their outflows was indeed the problem, the course of the conversation changed dramatically. If you've read any of the other blogs we've written about business and operations, or read any other business resource material, you will know that profit is a primary directive. Between calculated risk and reckless decision-making lies the dividing line between profit and loss. Show a lender you can make a profit through good decision-making and the process of getting a loan will be much easier.

Adding New Revenue Streams

(Would You Like Fries with That?)

I have never spoken to a Business Owner that was not looking to increase Revenue. Generally, they are looking to just increase the sales of their present offering, but the smart ones are looking to sell additional items to their existing clientele through up-sell, down-sell, and cross-sell. Let's break these concepts down for more clarification.

An Up-Sell is simply getting your customer to investigate the premium product or service with greater value than the product that they were looking at. Upselling can also be an added package to the original product that gives the selection more value. A simple example is, "would you like to make that a meal?", a familiar offer made by a well-known fast-food purveyor. The Down-Sell is used when your customer won't buy the primary product or service, so you offer a lower cost alternative. Now, the Cross-Sell is a related product or service, sometimes produced by another company (but not necessarily), that you can bolt on to the existing sale or sell to a past customer. Another simple example is, as the title of this blog has mentioned, "would you like fries with that?".

So, what are the considerations when diversifying your product or service offering? For me, adding additional revenue streams including the concepts of up-sell and cross-sell comes down to two primary factors: profitability and resources. Obviously, we cannot offer something that does not add to our bottom-line, therefore pricing is a very important calculation thereby ensuring that we have covered cost, cost of sale, and company overhead (or burden).

There are other ways to look at profitability though, such as "Loss-Leaders". They are customer convenience, or things that help you close a bigger deal. Imagine an ice cream store that doesn't offer toppings. Those toppings, profitable or not, help to sell the ice cream cone.

The other big consideration for me is the resources. Does adding this new product or service line capitalize on:

- Your existing customer base.
- The skills of your present staff, or does in require recruiting new skill set?
- Your present location
- The assets that produce the product that you presently own

If adding the revenue steam does not meet one or all these criteria, then serious and cautious thought should go into the following:

- Are we adding to our revenue or simply splitting our existing revenue between more offerings?

- If we have to find new customers for this new offering, where will they come from and how much will if cost to acquire them?
- Will I need additional space or expensive equipment?
- Would it be more cost effective to simply find more customers for the present offering?

If we are diversifying into new areas with new skills and equipment, I would treat that as a new business rather than a new revenue stream for this business. But finding ancillary products to sell that are related to your present offering and that your existing customers want, or need is a VERY smart business strategy.

Even better add-ons are the ones that come out of the waste within your present operation. For example; a lumber yard that makes a product from its sawdust or a baker that makes croutons from its day-old bread.

Adding revenue streams to your business can have several advantages and disadvantages. Some of the advantages include:
- Diversification of income sources
- Increased revenue
- Reduced risk of market volatility

On the other hand, some of the disadvantages include:
- Increased complexity in managing multiple revenue streams
- Increased costs associated with developing, storing, and maintaining new revenue streams
- Dilution of focus and resources
- Increased competition

For one thing, it is important to weigh the pros and cons before adding new revenue streams to your business. Also, to note, adding revenue streams should be done with caution and with careful consideration of the business's core competencies and resources. It is also important to ensure that the new revenue streams align with the business's overall strategy and goals. In any case, it makes sense to add revenue streams that compliment your core competencies and product/service line to stay focused in the marketing strategies that can and should be used to attract a greater client base. Most importantly, adding a revenue steam that, through financial analysis you determine costs you more than you are generating in revenue, makes no sense.

To simplify this concept, would you sell a product or service for $10 if it costs you $11 to produce it? Of course not. But as we have stated repeatedly in building and running your business effectively, "if you treasure it, you should measure it". Do the math, determine your true costs and a reasonable price that is profitable for you and remains appealing to your market.

Bootstrapping Your Business 23

You may have heard stories of a poor hungry child who buys a bottle of water for 30 cents and sells it for a dollar on the street, then buys two bottles and sells them, then more and more until he has a thriving business. Or the man that starts with a paperclip and continually makes trades until he owns a car and eventually a house.

These are extreme examples of "Bootstrapping" and when looked at from a business perspective, the success of these relatively small enterprises is extraordinary, not only in the achievement, but also in the lack of debt that they carry, and the simplicity in which they run.

Bootstrapping a business is the process of starting and growing a company with very limited resources. A bootstrap entrepreneur will often rely on their personal finances to get started, instead of investment from venture capital firms or angel investors. Bootstrapping can be an option for some business models with low costs or self-sustaining processes. It can also be a practice of funding growth with the business's own capital. Bootstrapping can provide autonomy but also challenges. Some of the advantages of bootstrapping are:

- You have more control over your business decisions and vision
- You do not have to share your profits or equity with investors
- You can focus on satisfying your customers and generating revenue
- You can be more flexible and agile in responding to market changes
- You can build a loyal and committed team that shares your passion

Some of the challenges of bootstrapping are:

- You may face financial risk
- You may have limited resources and opportunities for growth
- You may have to sacrifice your personal life and well-being
- You may have to deal with competition from well-funded rivals
- You may have to learn many skills and wear many hats

If you want to bootstrap your business, you need to have a clear vision, a viable product, a lean operation, a profitable business model, and a loyal customer base. You also need to be creative, resourceful, diligent, and resilient. Some examples of successful bootstrapped businesses are GoPro, Facebook, and Amazon. They all started with humble beginnings and grew into billion-dollar companies.

The term "sweat equity" comes to mind as these entrepreneurs may have lacked capital but made up for it with their extraordinary effort and determination. Whether using Bootstrapping to start a business, or to grow the business the lesson offers the same advice: take what you have in abundance. Example may include, but are not limited to:

- Good Ideas
- Special Skill(s)
- Excess Inventory
- Smart People
- Great Location(s)
- Abundant Connections
- Valuable Intellectual Property

And turn it into what you need, like:

- Cash
- Inventory
- Sales

Bootstrapping is the very essence of business in its most simple form, but sometimes we forget how simple it should be in order to work properly. We needlessly complicate our business with unproven expenses, partners who are not personally invested, employees needs/wants, and government compliance and thereby lose sight of the very thing that makes our business successful.

As we near the end of our first season of Biz Easy Podcasts, I think it is important to remind ourselves that we have an obligation to keep our business focused on the simple things that make the business work profitably and remember that everything else is just noise that distracts us from our mission.

The lessons of Bootstrapping should apply to ALL businesses, even the ones with deep pockets and plenty of resources. All businesses have an obligation to make as large a profit as is practical. That is achieved by eliminating waste and bringing in every sale possible. Every minute dealing with the "noise" takes us one step further from our mission.

Keep it Biz Easy and Lemon Squeezy

A Little About Your Authors

Skip Williams

Personal Motto:

"I shall not want for myself anything that I do not want for everyone. I am not worthy of a dime if I can not deliver at least a dollar's worth of value. I will do all that I can do each and every day to move myself and my clients closer to their goals. I believe in abundance, the more wealth we create for ourselves in turn creates more wealth for others."

Skip is a twice published author and a recognized speaker in business start-up and business improvement areas of expertise. With over twenty-five (25) years of experience in the Management, Financial Development & Operational fields he brings those years of analytical businesses to creating processes to successfully operate most modern business types.

Mr. Williams has been involved in the development of well over 800 businesses throughout the US, Canada, and the Caribbean working with owners, planners, operators, and potential owners. His approach is to study, analyze, educate, implement, and cultivate both small and large-scale projects. Skip is also known for his unique Computerized Business Model called "Financial Blueprint" that allows for financial analyses and feasibility studies.

Steve McCrillis
Personal Motto:

"People may not always believe what you say, but they will never doubt what you do."

Steve and his wife Tara have been residents of Tennessee since 2020 having moved there from Las Vegas (by way of San Diego). Having lived most of his life in Wisconsin, he graduated Magna Cum Laude with an undergraduate degree in Business Administration and has two Graduate Certifications attending Marquette University and Cardinal Stritch University in Milwaukee. After a successful career in retail management as VP of Sales and Operations, he decided that entrepreneurship was an avenue well worth the effort. Having planned, opened and grew his business before selling it years later, he then worked in small business analytics for 15 years until he passed the series 7, series 66 working in the Financial Securities industry as Financial Advisor with a focus on small business investment strategies.

Having visited over 3,900 small businesses across 50 states, Steve settled in Small Business Optimization and Strategic Planning for start-up and small business owners. Inspired by the perseverance and dedication required by those who choose to start and operate their own business, Steve has partnered with a like-minded professional with a congruent passion. Together with their team of professionals from the industry, Steve as a Principal with Resources & Development has been building relationships with small business owners in turn-around strategies, revenue generation and profit enhancement processes. Working as a collective body, their team is effectively suited to provide guidance, mentoring and education to small businesses nationwide.

The Biz Easy Podcast

The Biz Easy Podcast is an arm of Resources & Development. Since 2003 Resources & Development has worked with overworked, underpaid business owners to dramatically increase profits for their small or medium size business.

Being a business owner can be a lonely and often thankless job. You wear many hats, most of which you have the expertise for, and some that you may not. Sometimes vendors, employees, and even customers demand that they become your first priority and no one is looking out for you. And even though we may tell you some things you don't want to hear from time to time, this only works if WE ARE on your side.

At Resources & Development we want help build a better battleplan. One that prioritizes which next step will yield the greatest results and deliver additional profits that provide a healthy ROI on your investment in our fees as well as the incredible investment in time, moneys, and efforts that you have already made.

Whether you need more profit/money, more time, or a better quality of life, we are here to help.

Let us provide you with a **FREE test drive** and a step by step process to realize your goals. Visit us on the web for more information.

Resources-Development.com

For More Follow the Biz Easy Podcast:
https://www.youtube.com/@bizeasypodcast6263

Or Visit us online to connect with our podcast
and additional resources to help make
your worklife...Biz Easy.
https://resources-development.com/

www.ingramcontent.com/pod-product-compliance
Lightning Source LLC
Chambersburg PA
CBHW062334290526
45794CB00005B/2031